All Sort
of Art

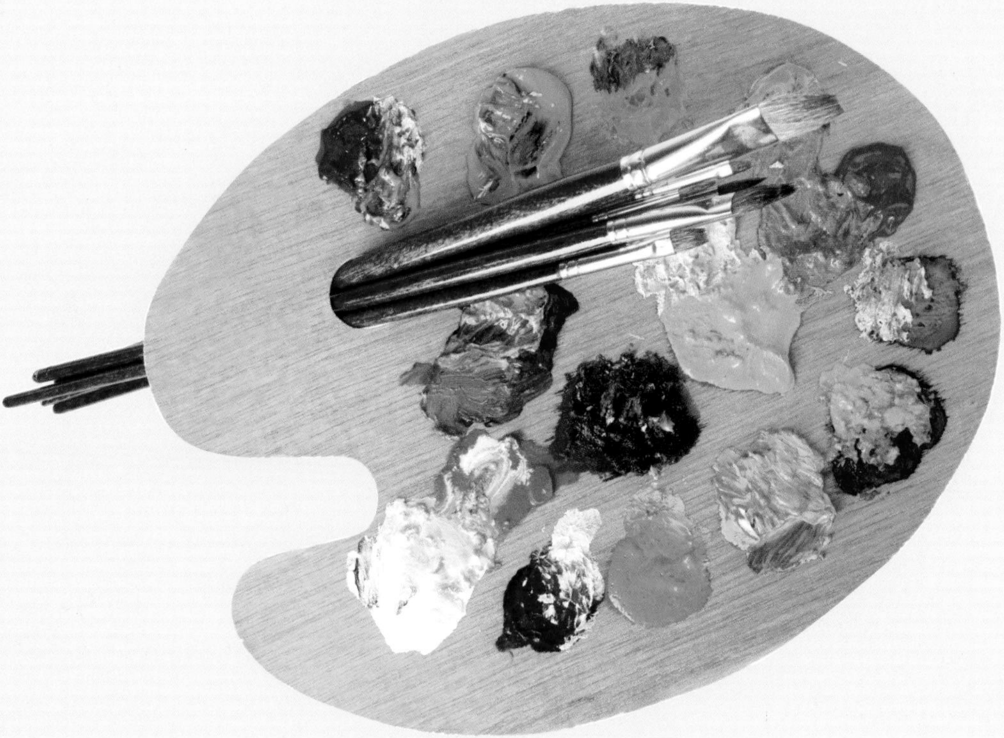

Written by Kathryn Stewart

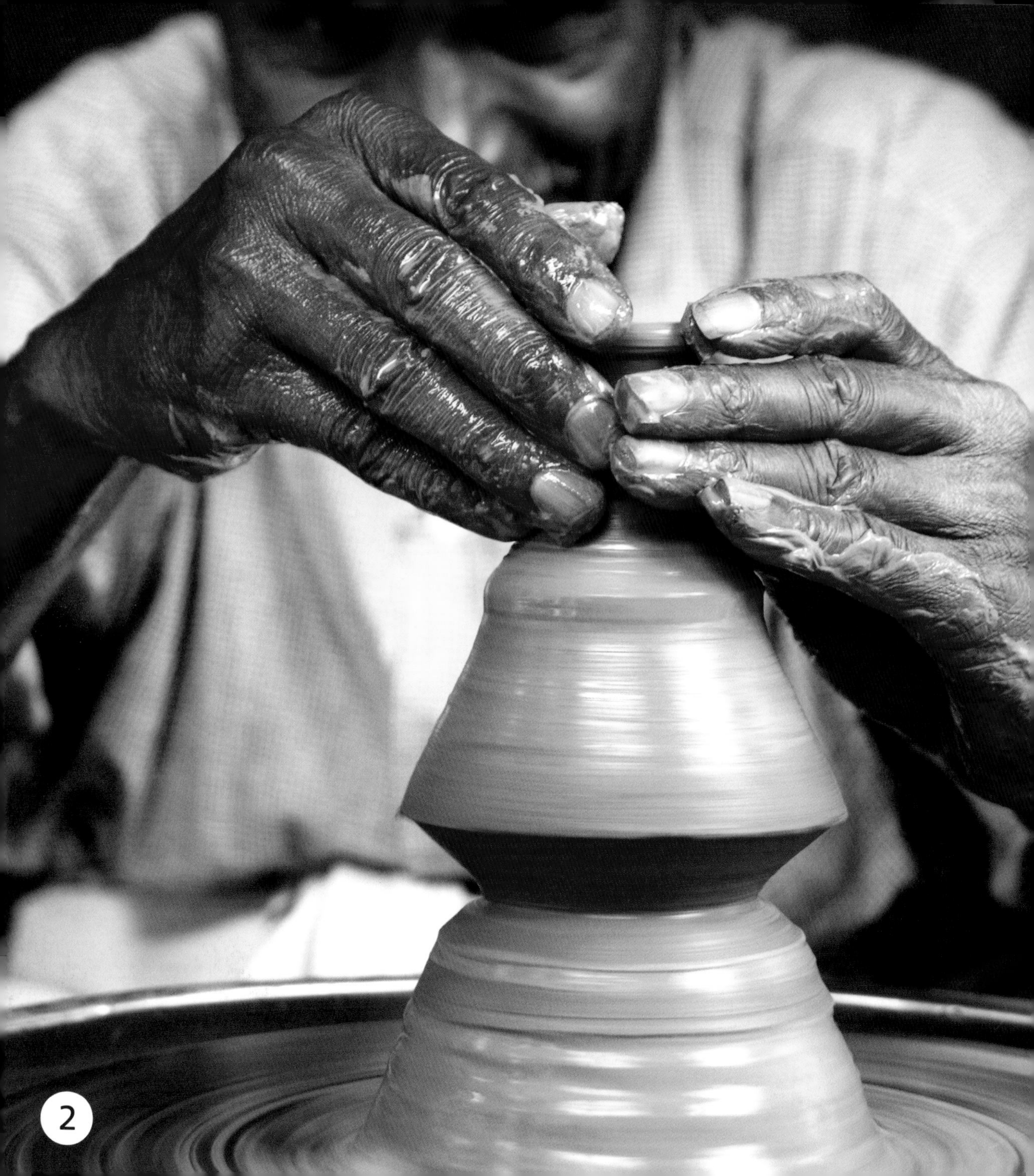

2

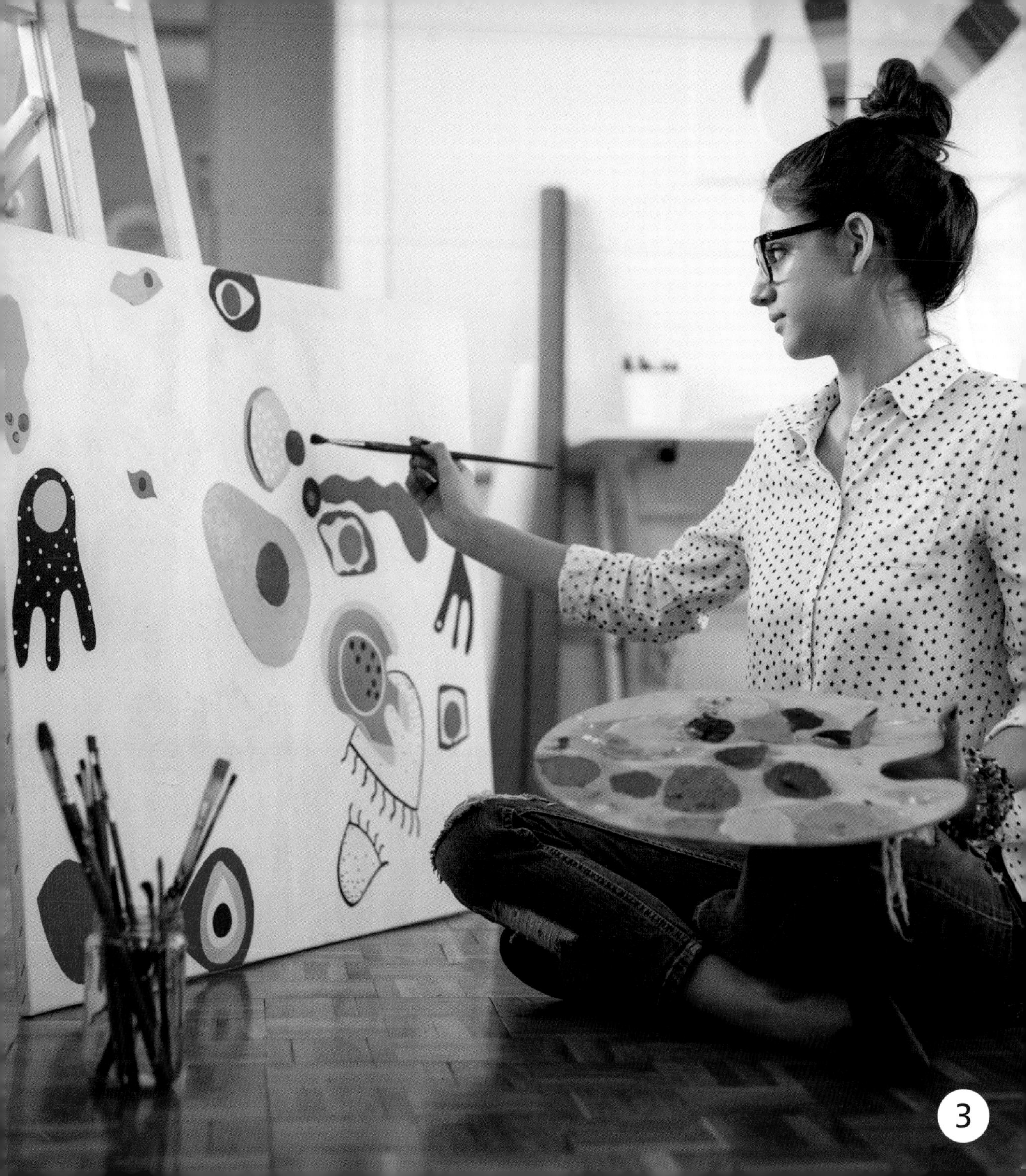

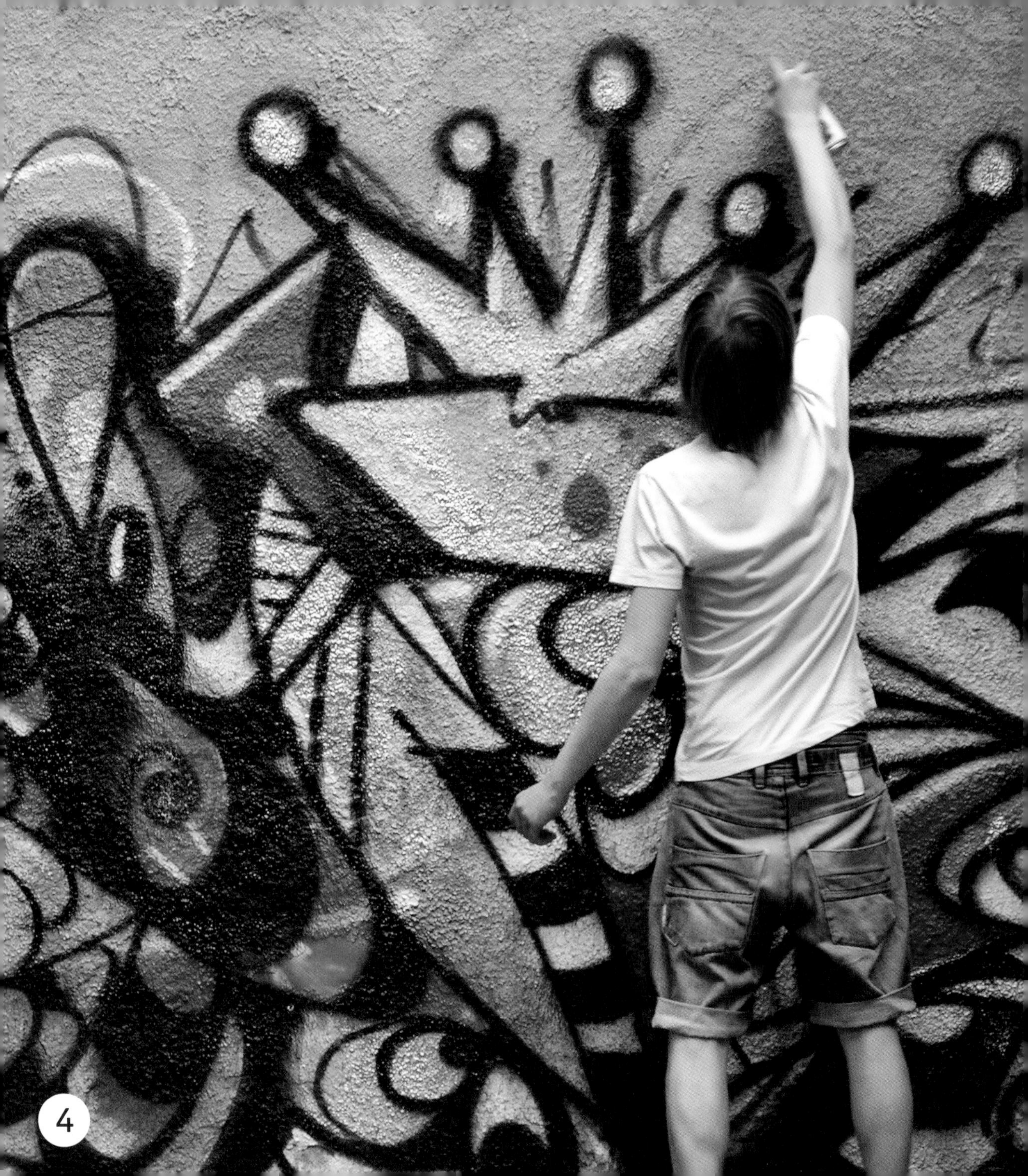

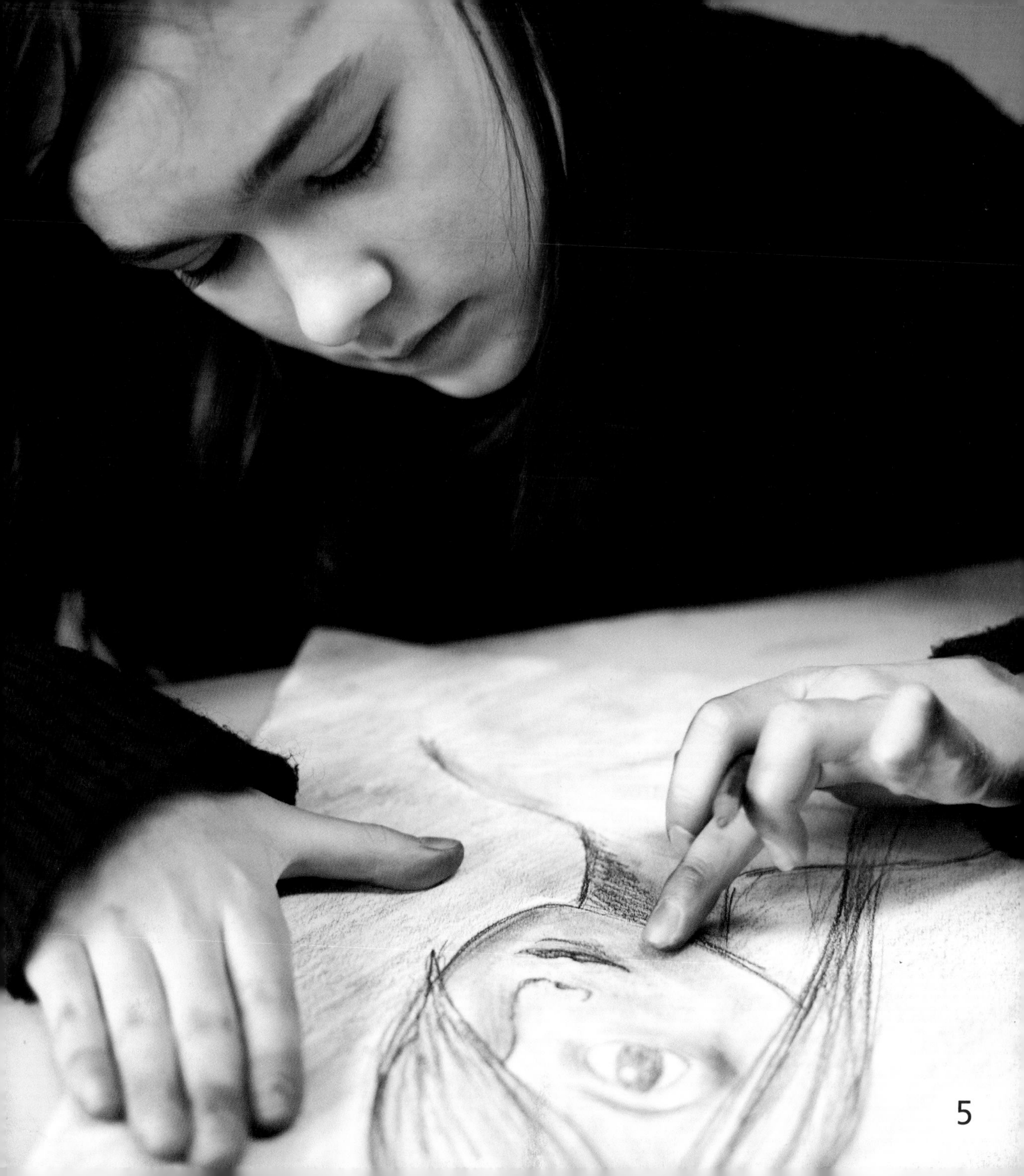

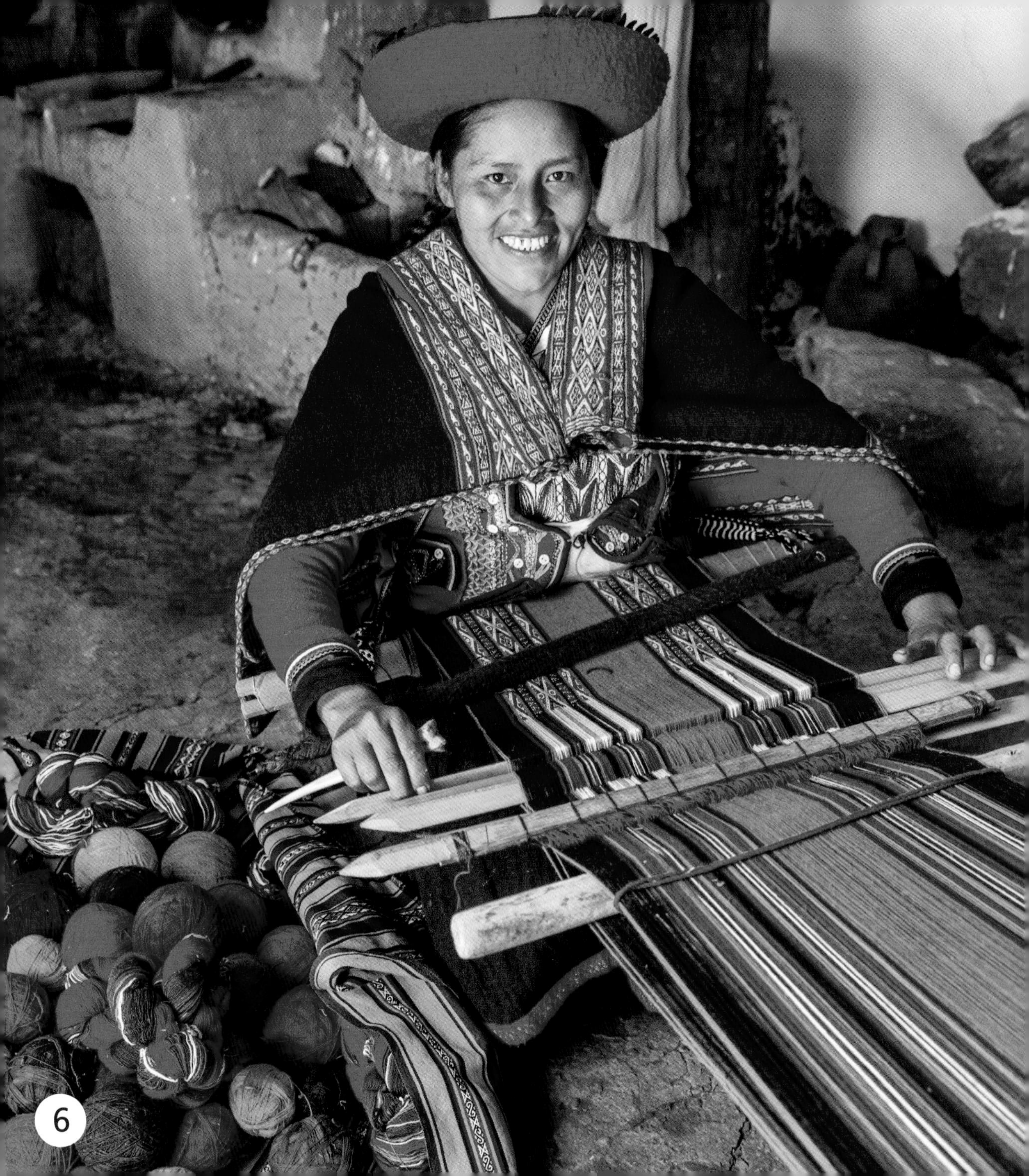

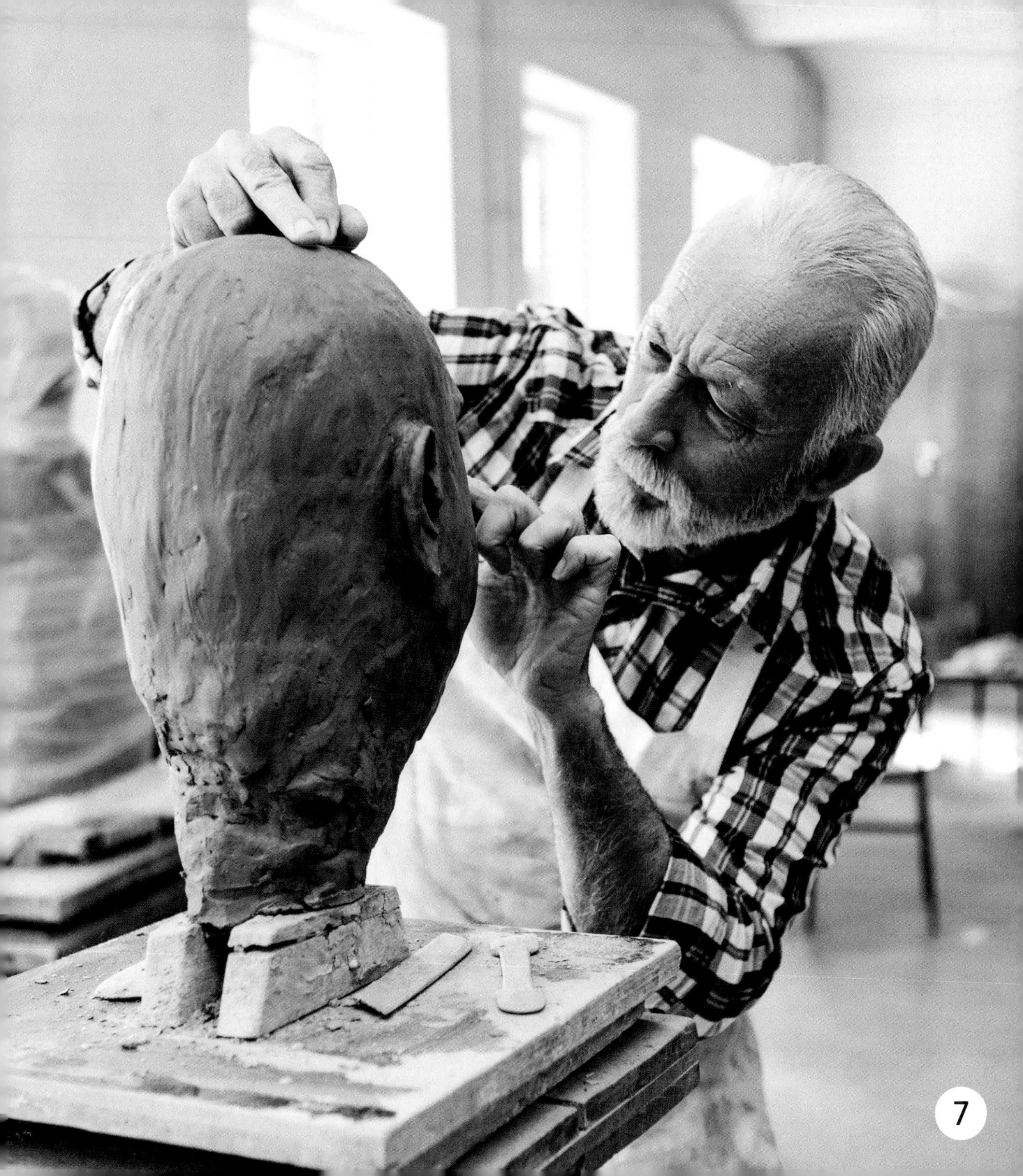

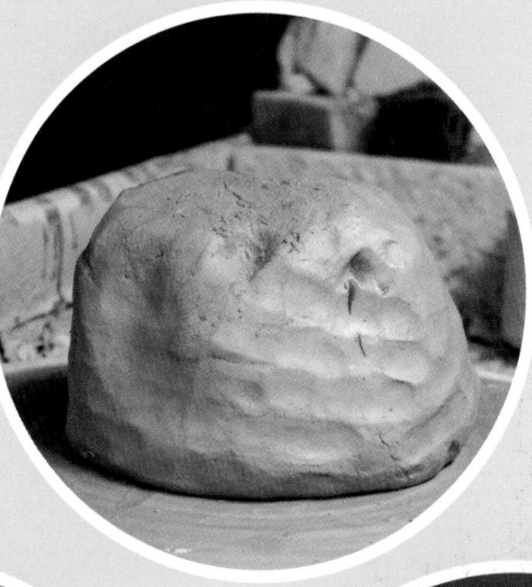
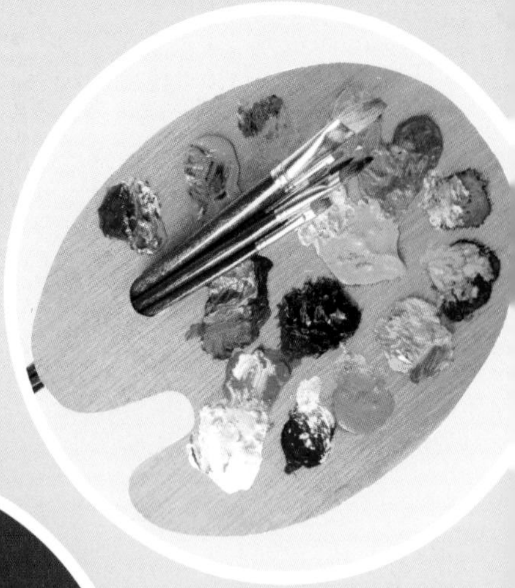
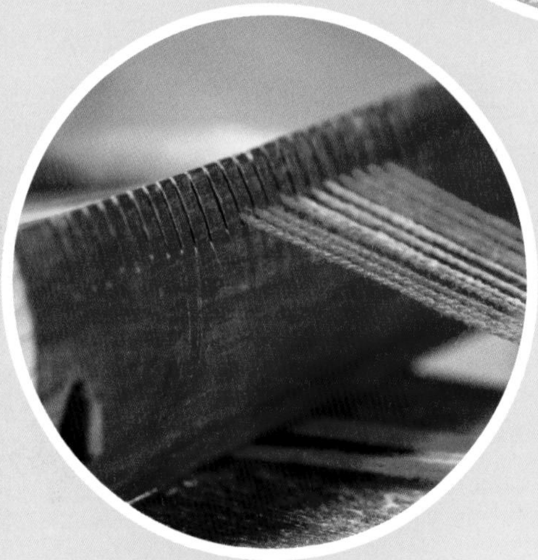
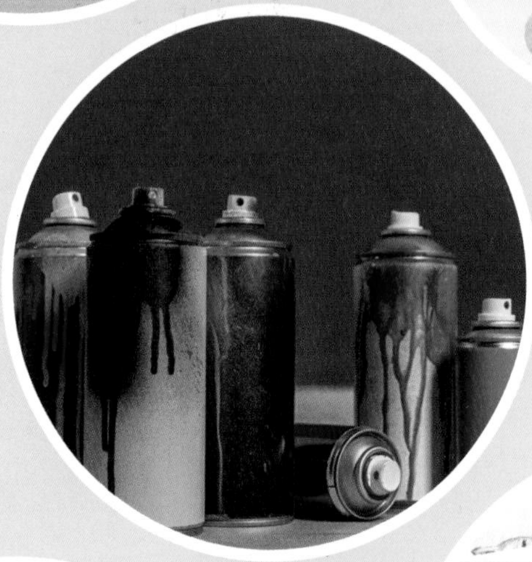
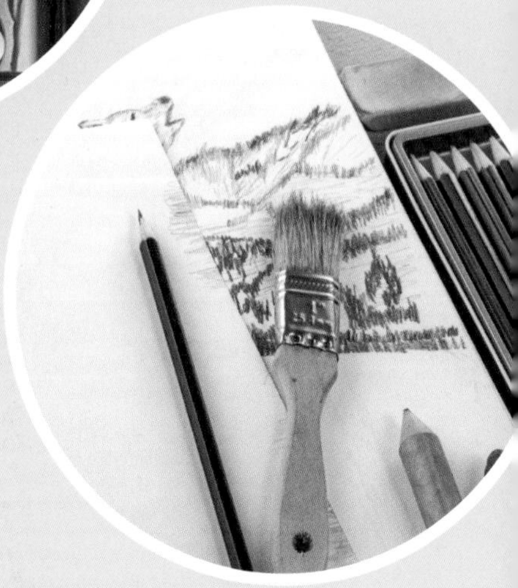
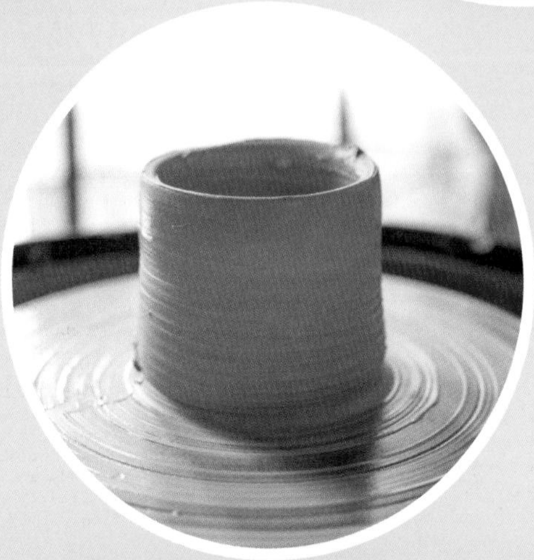